by Victor Gentle and Janet Perry

Gareth Stevens Publishing
A WORLD ALMANAC EDUCATION GROUP COMPANY

Please visit our web site at: www.garethstevens.com
For a free color catalog describing Gareth Stevens' list of high-quality books and multimedia programs, call 1-800-542-2595 (USA) or 1-800-461-9120 (Canada). Gareth Stevens Publishing's Fax: (414) 332-3567.

Library of Congress Cataloging-in-Publication Data

Gentle, Victor.
    Chasing sharks / by Victor Gentle and Janet Perry.
      p. cm. — (Sharks: an imagination library series)
    Includes bibliographical references and index.
    ISBN 0-8368-2825-9 (lib. bdg.)
     1. Sharks—Research—Juvenile literature. [1. Sharks.
  2. Shark fishing.] I. Perry, Janet, 1960- II. Title.
  QL638.9.G3583   2001
  597.3—dc21   00-052249

First published in 2001 by
Gareth Stevens Publishing
A World Almanac Education Group Company
330 West Olive Street, Suite 100
Milwaukee, WI 53212 USA

Text: Victor Gentle and Janet Perry
Page layout: Victor Gentle, Janet Perry, and Scott Krall
Cover design: Scott Krall
Series editor: Heidi Sjostrom
Picture Researcher: Diane Laska-Swanke

Photo credits: Cover, © Tim Calver/Innerspace Visions; p. 5 © Ron & Valerie Taylor/Innerspace Visions; pp. 7, 11 © Dr. Samuel Gruber/Innerspace Visions; p. 9 © Mark Strickland/Innerspace Visions; pp. 13, 15, 17 © Doug Perrine/Innerspace Visions; p. 19 © Peter Kragh/Innerspace Visions; p. 21 © David Fleetham/Innerspace Visions

This edition © 2001 by Gareth Stevens, Inc. All rights reserved to Gareth Stevens, Inc. No part of this book may be reproduced, stored in a retrieval system, or transmitted in any form or by any means, electronic, mechanical, photocopying, recording, or otherwise without the prior written permission of the publisher except for the inclusion of brief quotations in an acknowledged review.

Printed in the United States of America

1 2 3 4 5 6 7 8 9 05 04 03 02 01

> *Front cover:* Marine biologists and other scientists use equipment that allow sharks to be studied while they are alive. In this photo, taken from underwater, a researcher and his student study a lemon shark in the Bahamas.

TABLE OF CONTENTS

Dead or Alive?	4
Lifesaving Killers?	6
Trash or Treasure?	8
Waste and Want	10
Weapons and Tools	12
Live and Learn	14
Learn and Let Live	16
Friendly Sharks?	18
Shark Smart	20
More to Read and View	22
Places to Write and Visit	22
Web Sites	23
Glossary and Index	24

Words that appear in the glossary are printed in **boldface** type the first time they occur in the text.

DEAD OR ALIVE?

People who chase sharks think of the sharks in different ways.

Some people who catch fish see sharks as just cold-blooded killing machines to be caught for sport. Some fishers want to make money by selling the parts of sharks. According to most of these fishers, killing sharks is all right, even in very large numbers.

Marine biologists, however, see sharks as smart, sensitive, skillful **predators**. According to scientists, it is best to watch sharks, learn about them, and keep as many of them alive as possible.

This white shark is biting an outboard motor. Just before they capture food, white sharks close their eyes and depend on other senses. The **magnetic field** of the motor has confused the shark.

LIFESAVING KILLERS?

Dead or alive, no matter how you think of them, sharks are useful.

All parts of a dead shark can be used. Some parts can be eaten, some parts can be used for medicine, some parts make very strong leather, and some parts make sharp cutting tools.

Shark skeletons are made of **cartilage**, the same tough stuff that makes your nose and ears stiff but flexible. Certain **chemicals** in shark cartilage might be the reason that sharks never get cancer — and those chemicals could help cure human cancer.

A shark's **liver** is full of a special oil that could be used to help prevent heart disease.

Shark liver oil tablets, shark fin soup, and shark jerky are some of the extremely expensive things made from sharks.

TRASH OR TREASURE?

Shark skin is used for polishing wood and metal and for making fine leather clothing and furniture coverings. Shark teeth are used to make sharp weapons and cutting tools. Shark meat is a fine and nutritious food.

So you might wonder why some fishers kill sharks and then throw them out. Don't they know that catching even one shark means that they've found treasure?

If a shark is going to be killed, shouldn't most of its parts at least be used?

Someone removed the fins from this shark and then threw it back into the ocean, probably still alive. What cruelty! More than twenty dinners could have been made from this shark. What a waste of food!

WASTE AND WANT

After a sport fishing contest, people might take out the jaws of a shark they caught and keep them for a trophy. But most sharks caught at tournaments are trashed. How much food, medicine, and clothing could come from the sharks near the garbage truck in this picture?

Sometimes, to avoid killing more sharks, scientists use sharks from fishing contests for scientific study. Then at least some of the sharks aren't wasted.

Scientists look inside shark stomachs to see what sharks eat. They take apart shark eyes, brains, hearts, and other parts of the body to see how sharks work. They also look inside **pregnant** sharks to see how baby sharks develop.

All these sharks, caught in a fishing tournament for prize money, were wasted. In some places, shark meat sells for about $20 a plate. How much money was lost by the contest winners?

WEAPONS AND TOOLS

Sharks are usually pretty strong, and most fight hard to get away if they are caught.

Some fishers use modern and sometimes painful tools to hunt sharks and kill them: big boats, **sonar**, large and small hooks, nets, guns, and sticks.

Scientists are hunters too, in a way. They hunt sharks to examine and learn more about them. Yet, their tools are specially made to keep the sharks alive.

Because most sharks won't stay alive in aquariums, scientists have to study sharks where sharks live. So scientists use computers, **radar**, magnets, and special underwater diving equipment to chase sharks and capture them. Then they release the sharks — alive.

This lemon shark has a radio in it that sends information to the monitor (the domed thing on the ocean floor). A computer somewhere else collects the information.

LIVE AND LEARN

Using computers, marine biologists collect information on where sharks travel every year, how much energy they use to stay alive, and what upsets them and disturbs their normal behavior.

Using radar and **magnetic pulses** sent through the water, scientists now know that sharks follow magnetic fields that they "feel" in the water. Sharks know what's happening miles (km) away from them. Sharks are really much more sensitive than we ever realized.

Because of modern equipment, we can learn about the world of these mysterious and powerful animals without damaging a single one.

Near the boat a magnet sends pulses through the water to see if sharks change direction when the pulses are on. This would show if sharks find their way using Earth's magnetic field.

LEARN AND LET LIVE

Underwater cameras, special shark-diving suits, and deep-sea devices make it possible to chase sharks in a whole new way — without becoming a tasty shark snack. After watching sharks with this new equipment, scientists had to admit that even the experts are sometimes wrong.

We used to think that sharks traveled alone. We also thought that if sharks stopped swimming, they would stop breathing.

Because of new diving equipment, we have learned that nurse, reef, and horn sharks often stop swimming and rest in underwater caves with groups of their own species.

Only a short time ago, diving equipment became light and easy to move. Without it, no one would know that reef sharks rest in caves in groups, much less be able to pet one.

FRIENDLY SHARKS?

It's also not true that the only reason that lone sharks gather in groups is for a **feeding frenzy** — where each shark greedily snatches chunks of a large kill before it can be eaten by other sharks.

We now know that sharks gather in groups to hunt better — and for other reasons. Some dogfish sharks hunt together, then share their kill. **Scalloped** hammerhead sharks meet by the hundreds in spring. Scientists aren't sure why they gather this way, but it's not for food. Maybe they just like to hang out with their buddies!

Groups of a hundred or more scalloped hammerheads school near Mexico. Scientists don't know why, because equipment quiet enough to observe their actions hasn't yet been developed.

SHARK SMART

Humans have taken many hundreds of years just to make the right tools to find out the truth about sharks. We had to get smart enough to learn how wonderful sharks are!

Sharks are **immune** to cancer, easily find their way in the ocean, and sense fish hundreds of miles away.

Before scientists had learned all this, it was easy to think that sharks were simply stupid and mean. But now that we understand more about sharks, how should we behave toward them? Is it all right to kill them for sport and throw them out? Is it all right to kill them for food, medicine, clothing, and tools? Or should we just study them alive — and learn more about all life in the ocean?

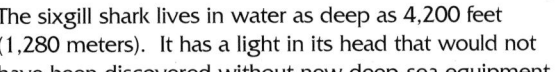

The sixgill shark lives in water as deep as 4,200 feet (1,280 meters). It has a light in its head that would not have been discovered without new deep-sea equipment.

MORE TO READ AND VIEW

Books (Nonfiction) *Eugenie Clark: Adventures of a Shark Scientist.* Ellen R. Butts and Joyce R. Schwartz (Shoe String Press)
Eyewitness Activity File: Shark. Deni Bown (DK Publishing)
Informania Sharks. Informania (series). C. Maynard (Candlewick)
A Look Inside Sharks and Rays. Keith Banister (Reader's Digest)
Real Kids, Real Adventures #1: Shark Attack. Deborah Morris (Bookpartners)
Shark Magic for Kids. Animal Magic for Kids (series). Patricia Corrigan (Gareth Stevens)
Sharks (series). Victor Gentle and Janet Perry (Gareth Stevens)

Books (Fiction) *Shark Bites: True Tales of Survival.* Greg Ambrose (Island Bookshelf)
The Shark Callers. Eric Campbell (Harcourt Brace)

Videos (Nonfiction) *Hunt for the Great White Shark.* (National Geographic)
National Geographic's Really Wild Animals: Deep Sea Dive. (National Geographic)
Vanishing Wonders of the Sea. (Sumeria)

PLACES TO WRITE AND VISIT

Here are three places to contact for more information:

Greenpeace
702 H Street NW
Washington, DC 20001
USA
1-202-462-1177
www.greenpeace.org

World Wildlife Fund
1250 24th Street NW, Suite 500
Washington, DC 20037
USA
1-800-CALL-WWF
www.wwf.org

Vancouver Aquarium
P.O. Box 3232
Vancouver, BC
Canada V6B 3X8
1-604-659-3474

To find a zoo or aquarium to visit, check out www.aza.org and, on the American Zoo and Aquarium's home page, look under AZA Services, and click on Find a Zoo or Aquarium.

WEB SITES

If you have your own computer and Internet access, great! If not, most libraries have Internet access. The Internet changes every day, and web sites come and go. We believe the sites we recommend here are likely to last, and that they give the best and most appropriate links for our readers to pursue their interest in sharks and their environment.

www.ajkids.com
This is the junior Ask Jeeves site — it's a great research tool. Some questions to try out in Ask Jeeves Kids:
> What do we know about sharks' senses?
> Which sharks are most endangered?

You can also just type in words and phrases with "?" at the end, for example:
> Shark conservation?
> Shark products?

www.mbayaq.org/lc/kids_place/kidseq.asp
This is the Kids' E-quarium of the Monterey Bay Aquarium. Make postcards, print out coloring pages, play games, go on a virtual deep-sea dive, or find out about some marine science careers.

oberon.educ.sfu.ca/splash/tank.htm
It's the Touch Tank. Click on a critter or a rock in the aquarium to see more about it.

www.pbs.org/wgbh/nova/sharks/world/clickable.html
It's the Clickable Shark. Click on any part of the shark picture to find out how sharks work.

kids.discovery.com/KIDS
Click on the Live SharkCam. See a live leopard shark and live blacktip reef sharks!

artcontext.com/~ocean/home/html
The Ocean of Know web page is supported by the Mote Marine Laboratory. Click on Sharks. Then click on Shark Tagging Learning Activity for really neat shark science in action.

www2.orbit.net.mt/sharkman.htm
Enter the Sharkman's World near Malta. He's a scuba diver who is completely soaked in anything even a little bit sharky. You'll find poetry, music, and shark pictures there. The Sharkman is not a scientist, but he loves to talk sharks with other shark fans — like you!

www.pbs.org/wgbh/nova/sharks/world/whoswho.html
Here's a shark "family tree." Click on any of the titles, and you'll see what kinds of sharks belong in the same group, and why. If you see a picture of a shark you don't know, use the Shark-O-Matic to get answers.

GLOSSARY

You can find these words on the pages listed. Reading a word in a sentence helps you understand it even better.

cartilage (KAR-till-ij) — flexible but stiff support tissue, like bone but softer 6

chemicals (KEM-i-kuls) — substances that join together to make up all things 6

feeding frenzy (FEE-ding FREN-zee) — a group of animals eating in a violent and very excited way 18

immune (ih-MYUN) — protected from ever catching a certain disease 20

liver (LIH-ver) — an organ in many animals that helps cleanse the blood of wastes 6

magnetic field (mag-NEH-tik FEELD) — an area of invisible forces around electrical currents and some metals; shark sense organs can feel magnetic fields 4, 14

magnetic pulses (mag-NEH-tik PULS-iz) — short magnetic bursts of power 14

marine biologists (mar-EEN bi-OL-uh-jists) — scientists who study life in the water 4, 14

predators (PREH-duh-ters) — animals that hunt other animals for food 4

pregnant (PREG-nint) — having babies growing inside 10

radar (RAY-dar) — a machine that bounces radio waves off shapes to find them 12, 14

scalloped (SKAL-upt) — edged with a row of side-by-side half circles 18

sonar (SO-nar) — a tool to find underwater objects by bouncing sound off of them 12

INDEX

cancer 6, 20

diving 12, 16

equipment 12, 14, 16, 18, 20

feeding frenzies 18

fins 6, 8, 10

fishing 2, 4, 8, 10, 12

magnetic fields 4, 14

medicine 6, 10, 20

radar 12, 14

scientists 4, 10, 12, 14, 16, 18, 20

senses 4, 14, 20

shark meat 6, 8, 10

shark skin 8

shark teeth 8

sonar 12

tournaments 10

uses of sharks 6, 8, 10, 14, 20